Era's End

poems by

Elaine Zimmerman

Finishing Line Press
Georgetown, Kentucky

Era's End

Publisher: Leah Huete de Maines
Editor: Christen Kincaid
Cover Art: Hannah Zimmerman
Author Photo: Hannah Zimmerman
Cover Design: Elizabeth Maines McCleavy

Order online: www.finishinglinepress.com
also available on amazon.com

Author inquiries and mail orders:
Finishing Line Press
PO Box 1626
Georgetown, Kentucky 40324
USA

Contents

Lullaby During Insurrection
January 6, 2021

My cheek on the back of your head,
I hold my breath to be sure yours
is still there, in and out, in and out.
So small, I cup your foot as if how
we stand begins in our hands.

Your fingers grasp my hair and neck.
We rest, heart against heart. A painting
of immigrants, just left of the piano,
across from where we sit. Like you,
they came through a rough, long climb.

Now safe and buoyed by one another,
moon meets them in shade and light.
A tree climbs to sky should they need a
bough to lift them forward or to different
harbor. I take them in, while you sleep.

Afraid to move just an inch. One shift
of hip or chin, and soft cradling breaks
open like a cloud. Outside our window,
fir branch glistens in ice. Taps and bends
toward us. Patches of snow float down.

A flock of geese crosses over. Trumpet-loud,
as if wild cries might warn and upend tumult.
Fiercely they protect a vast sky that covers
our new-found sleep; tents what will come
next, when we first wake.

Last Ten Days of August, 2021

The cow is stuck in a tree, wedged between branches. Swept away
by floodwaters after Hurricane Ida made landfall. Workers from
St. Bernard Parish use chainsaws to help her land.

US military board the last departure. The contract working dogs,
trained to sniff out bombs in Kabul, are left behind. Not protected,
they'll likely get new handlers.

The groom's father does not show up for wedding photos. But his
wife gets him onto the dance floor, one special time. A foxtrot.
Later, he buys two guns; refuses to get immunized.

The youth counselor stores supplies and food in his basement.
Sleeps there, in a blue hammock. Prepares for the worst and buys
special gear. Lots of stored water.

Vietnamese workers sleep in tents on factory floor to reduce COVID
spread and protect the supply chain. So fragile now, one accident and
flow splinters like cracked glass.

The Governor, on his last day in Albany, asks if anyone will keep his
Siberian shepherd, Captain, with a nipping personality. No one on
staff offers. It's not clear what happens next.

Port congestion is like heart congestion. Slowed down, obstruction
in the pathways. The cost of magnets in puzzle toys has risen 50%
since March. Better start buying now for Christmas.

Local news—"Was it from the storm? Anybody else notice dead
birds? I have a large tree in my front yard. Came out and found
multiple dead birds. Almost like they fell out to their death."

Pilot lowers the plane for more oxygen. A passenger in labor—
between countries—fleeing Taliban. In the cargo bay of the aircraft,
a newborn breathes, opens her eyes.

Echo of Stone

for Nelba Marquez-Greene

The daughter is winging wildly
against the white orchards.
Braided hair, braided dusk.

The hills shift and fold in
ebbing light. A blue line
ribbons through memory.

The mother sobs.
Nothing but shattered urns.
Her daughter shot. Gone.

Where did we forget our wholeness?
Wanting the holes in her daughter's fabric
to grow roots of purpose. Hair, limb, vine.

Open the skin. We sleep in dust.
Tear the pulp. Nothing is changed.
Repeat the end. An echo of stone.

Please, hold the roof down; guard
the light. Fold arms around each child
and what shoots forth from clay.

Do not ignore our small and vast despair.
A whisper of wings,
as close to us as breathing.

Each lamb returns slowly down the path.
The shepherd counts with rod of ash.
Through a dark window, the mother stares.

Twirls her son's curls. The night
a long knife, sharp as what pierces
through dirt air sound breath.

Found

The dog howls as if on fire. A shrill sound waking
neighbors, small children under thick knit quilts.
Then an eerie silence. A calculated robbery; bloody
steak meat all over the floor. Everything cleaned out,
even the hound. Signs tacked on trees, iron gates.

Reward of one hundred dollars. Green coat dragging,
a tired woman walks up Planet Street. Wool hat
pushed down around the ears. Boots too large, but
thick bottoms, ribbed and safe on ice. She rarely falls
now. Tied together with rope, she pulls a dog along.

Someone dropped the mutt off at the shelter.
He jumps up, wags his tail for a pat on the head.
She doesn't mind. He keeps her warm, protects her.
What she would give to be found, returned with open arms.
No questions asked. "But here, here is your dog."

"Lucky you put the sign up in the place where I sit all day.
Sometimes you find something, but it's like a missing tooth.
Someone knocked it out. No one knows it belongs to you."
She turns away. One fifty and five tens in her pocket.
She'll get a turkey sandwich, pecan pie. Ask for it heated.

Leap, Fly, Sliver

Thick fog. Early morning drive.
A deer leaps in the mist
like memory, or the quick glance,
that changes everything.

Each year blue herons return to
their nineteen nests by the old
bridge and pond. Spread wings
in calligraphy, a letter in the sky.

We throw stones there. With each
toss and weight, ask forgiveness.
While the birds feed their young and
swans turn to cove with five in tow.

Worms sliver beneath wet rock. Curl and
turn. Wait for morning when dew tastes
young and light slants in. Unaware of
shape or line, their dance is simply breath.

Fox walks the field's edge. We watch.
Neighbors do, too. Pull in dogs and cats
as well as whatever living dreams are
small, but worth holding on to.

Cold Know-How

Sunday is only Sunday to those who
forget the order of pleading children
for bread and truth before daybreak.

Beneath the pile of leaves, a bone.
White arc of moon, stroke of sky.
Relentless silhouette.

If you linger, Milky Way breathes
down the neck into your palms.
Break open the bone, a talisman.

What comes out but the last dream
of a child who saw the village
rampaged. Thick legs, knives.

Shoulder to shoulder lies. Walk
over heads like soft flooring
of history. Ribbons in the mouth.

The ears hear corn; corn hears yellow.
Husk hears shedding; shed hears door.
Door hears stairs. Stairs hear between

the walls. The walls hear children,
climbing. Moon is lamp in the ceiling.
Small fingers hold a charm.

Smooth as a tooth under the pillow.
If truth is old shoes, then walk fast to
cold know-how. The cold hear knives.

The knowing hear why. The how
hear bones, cracked and forgotten.
What does forgotten sound like?

The Dogs Wear Shoes

The dogs wear shoes.
Their owners protect
parquet floors from
outdoor germs, whiffs
of loss. A tumbling of
leftovers pile up against
the town rail.

Streets smell of waste.
Some dog, some human.
A few men pull down
their pants midday.
Rot and fear in mouth.
Nothing left to hide.
Day-old bread. One plum.

Empty bus stop. Opened
trash. Locket in left pocket.
Counting days years.
What is remembered
outside of the kinder
inside ways? Lull and
hum, the toddler sings.

Says hello to a man
lying on the sidewalk.
Her father says no. She
leaves a treat for the man.
Pretends it's for the dog.
Has already learned how to
deceive, so she can care.

What Was Left

Post bed on lawn. Stained glass window
casts a story. Glowing and textured with
polished edges. Dutch doors, bold yellow
and magenta. Whether you open top or
bottom, it's still a junkyard. Lit up with
what was once hope, now traced in lines
more costly than crime. Why she would
sell her right kidney, if only she had one.

Sea glass in jar on the vanity. Pink, aqua,
soft hue of white lies, plucked from shore.
Tumble of broken mussels and small stone
shine. Slim petticoats. Lace hemlines.
Red leather boots polished up for dancing.
She powders on rouge. Sweet blush of
a smile. Light blue for the eyes. A bit
of pretense holds the day together.

If only someone would buy the fence posts.
All even and pointing, as if life were balanced,
fair and hammered in earth, protecting the
gardens from wild rootings. After Iraq, he
dreamed of things he could not say. Screams
each night, louder than her grabbing, pushing
down before the first birth. But there are no
babies now. Just gin, blades, loaded revolver.

At Paul's Redemption Center, he spits out
recovery. Like a rock in the mouth, too hard
to swallow. A new stutter, as if to say it,
talk it, would be to kill again. His breathing
trouble back. What wolf would turn this corner?
What bear would paw this heart? Two loops
in the sky; circling hawks close in on carnage.
A woman buys red boots, lace slip, some time.

Pandemic's Start—2020 Chronicle
First 100,000 deaths

| 3/23 | 522 deaths* |

Wind blows the bugs around.
Rain throws side walls of river
as air turns brown earth blue.

| 3/25 | 954 deaths |

Who to touch to dare?
Children scare on bike and stair.
Close it down. Shut the stores.

| 3/27 | 1,609 deaths |

Move city folk to suburb. $450.00
A quick job. But the lily pad is same
green same green same green.

| 3/31 | 3,902 deaths |

Fishing season. Glass eel turn a true
fortune. A new virus on the banks.
Gambling life for fast cash.

| 4/2 | 5,952 deaths |

Lonely-blue paper taped on window.
Dirty water-yellow sign tacked on door.
Color-coded notes for health workers.

| 4/4 | 8,535 deaths |

Homeless students, not turning
in their homework. "Ghost students,"
just plain missing.

4/6   10,984 deaths
Mask expired, but cleared for use.
Face marks, as if kicked.

4/8   14,737 deaths
Walk one side of road to the other.
No human contact.
Touch is fallen leaf on pond.

4/10   18,751 deaths
Eating alone with so many strangers.
The new bar. Round bite, sweet drizzle
of cream. Car line at the donut shop.

4/14   26,185 deaths
Farmers bury growth.
Plow beans back to soil.
Pour milk into manure pits.
Not enough customers.

4/18   34,689 deaths
Wiped out by fraudsters. Savings gone.
He thought they were advising him.
Where are the angels when wolves
are wearing face masks?

4/20   37,999 deaths
A 5 year old dies.
Her parents, first responders.

4/22   42,676 deaths
Traffic gone; new sounds.
Bees swarming, like a saw
slicing wind.   Listen.

4/26   49,255 deaths
Clap and spin—100th patient saved.
Drumming pans for health workers.

4/28   52,482 deaths
The EMT, 23, used his father's gun.
Too much, too fast.

4/30   57,406 deaths
Blood pressure in a tailspin.
Tornado of the heart.
The body is the nation.

5/2   60,782 deaths
Pulling out what held them on.
Tubes left inside so many patients.
Funeral directors, the last responders.

5/4   62,887 deaths
His hope for a new kidney dashed.
No swimmers. Cars parked.
Fewer fresh accidents.

5/6   67,339 deaths
Blood memory. Choctaws sent food
to the Irish in the Great Famine.
The favor returns now.

5/10   80,320 deaths
Talking on screen in group.
No one sensed her relapse.

5/14   83,098 deaths
Damp. Cold. Bumping
shoulders. Shout to hear,
slicing bone. Knife the truth.
Meat cutters pack up.

5/18   84,739 deaths
Mask covers nurse's face.
She sings high spirit blues. Hums
on, holding his hand. The patient
gone, cradled in a stranger's song.

5/20   87,472 deaths
Grads high five in cap and gown.
No graduation, but photos at Town Hall.
Ambulance speeds by; beeps a loud cheer.
One paused ritual may slow another.

5/22   92,005 deaths
Orange and white body bags.
The dead may know to wait.
What if the lost are fallen heroes;
what marker, what wreath?

5/25   92,541 deaths
He can't breathe.
No respirator, no ventilator.
Knee on neck. 9 minutes.
We all fall down.

5/27   94,492 deaths
Bent in shock, in prayer.
His brother kneels, shudders.

5/29   96,963 deaths
Stunned hush becomes a roar.
The streets are veins burst open.

5/31   98,600 deaths
Shuttered cities wake.
In upswell, the nation is
the body, full lung and belly.

6/2   100,246 deaths
Thousands rush forward.
Sky, a vast thunder.
Startled truth, unmasked.

COVID Data Tracker, John Hopkins

The Ditch

Lincoln County, Mississippi, 1958

This is the stone from the river before
starlings shook the hickory with
worm and seed for open beaks.
This is the mud that tucked the fire
to feet and flight under an orange sky,
strips of coal drifting in cirrus white.

This is the ditch the children walked in.
A floor of spike and shard for games,
when water told nothing and dry was all.
This is the back and forth of boys.
A volley of scrap tossed one side to
another. Lifting up what's thrown away.

This is the car that raced towards them,
in a catch and throw of treasure troves
and high-pitched what's next laughter.
This is the man who eyed the boys.
Daughters in the back seat felt his rage,
like colts against the high-pasture fence.

This is the piece of glass they saw.
What nearly hit and scratched but then
a hand so close, split-second catch.
This is the line that breaks us.
The friend caught the shard to stop
the fate of young black boys in a ditch.

This is the hand that held the world
when a car swept by, past simple truth.
The bone so white, no doctor for healing.
This is the hand that keeps men alive.
The blood a river, a stone, a shaking of seed.
This is not the last time.

Emergency Room

My eyes sink into your eyes.
The sea full of awe and fear.
Lines break sky after sky.

Page after page, lost or
discarded. The true story
thrown overboard.

Fish search for food and light
in schools and swarm. Waves
thunder down. Blue on blue.

Night is all color. Day tints in
empty. Shards of loss and hue.
My eyes sink into your eyes.

Era's End

So much more than day or light
the sound of sea, breezing through.
Stones remember sheets of ice,
early falls; turn over, catching grace
or hail. Birch tremble, horned-owl hoots.

No one ever thought beginning here
would come to be. Yet here we are.
Knees trembling. Deer in the thicket.
A dream recalled. Something about gifts
in the balance of one person or many.

Red fox runs through the field, prey
dangling from his teeth. Poised in a dance
only the trapped tail and fox know.
We hike past, stung by miscalculation.
Our own catch tied to the hip.

Some have come to feed on us, as well.
They tiptoe by the dirt road, feathers
in their mouths; arms full of gifts.
How would you take this day?
The sea whines, a colt whinnies.

What else to do when what we hear and
sense is not a song, but gone to slow sorrow.
The underside of moss, thick with worm.
Only years will unravel this gnarled growth
and happenstance that took us by surprise.

To a Survivor

Open the shutters, just for a while.

Sounds scrape the years with songs
forgotten. A lyric from a different
country. The tunes of the enemy
belong to the Allies now. Listen.

No telling how lies became small hats
worn by children marching with dolls.
They carried small paper bags filled
with cake, rhyme and tricks.

Rooves spit rain; the jays drop seed.
Beneath yellow gourds, black ants
carve the center in thick patterned
lines. Quick, slip through the stairwell.

Climb gnarled vines. If only for daylight,
without fractured time. What was once
a small key is now a vast tree, shrouding
the lost, leafing through finds.

Open the shutters, just for a while.

On My Way to Coffee at 7:00 AM During COVID-19

A hook for a hand and rage that reaches farther than his missing arm, he walks toward me screaming, "You're the one I've wanted to kill for years." Piercing cries stack like waves. Echoes from a flogging. Lost shoe, ropes dragging. Flame in bone. His stare runs through time stomach spleen. I'm not the only one imagined dead for what came before. The morning jogger cornered by a truck in cat and mouse chase. Gunned down. He died alone; three watched, cursed his race. Asleep at home, the EMT hears the door come off its hinges. Search warrant for the wrong house, but 32 shots. She's done. No one checks her pulse for twenty minutes in the hallway. Knee on neck eight minutes long he pleads. Others cry for help. He calls to momma his final words; knows he's gone. Or mental health ignored, they put a spit hood over his head. Press face to pavement, cuffed and naked on public roadway. Off life supports, one week later. And the man in his car at a drive-thru, asleep at the wheel. Or the man at the dollar store and then one man after that. Did you know his name? You are what you do or don't do. Who said yes who said no, who stopped the noose? Did you report the man looking calmly at birds in upturned boughs? This city is burning. Some march some chant. Lids don't sit right on drinks or trash. Filthy choice of men trained to kill. Audacity of bone to power, hands in pockets. No one's safe. So many dying and dying so fast. Not enough room in morgues. The dead freeze in trucks. More body bags. Skin color zipped up. Beneath the walk, worms and moles wake to thunder. Windows shake. If glass shivers, this is the loudest whisper of what will soon break.

Pandemic Spring and Then What?

The groundhog does not see his shadow today but I give
you mine for the number of springs we missed together.
Buds will open in this season of mad flush and flood.

The wind does not still, but I do, sipping pause from a spoon.
Cars rock back and forth like cradles, unable to budge in the storm.
What moves the future when so much is stalled or gone?

Geese do not stop flying in vee formation. But I leave
the line, prefer moon pull me to prayer. Move
between waking and wonder, if wings have their way.

Night does not tire or whine, but I fall asleep dreaming of shoes,
something forgotten. Silver key tucked in the wrong drawer.
Was the light on before purpose slipped out like a thief?

Song does not linger in the throat, but I remember humming.
Small birds sip from puddles. Something purrs in the heart
for simpler tunes, each other in the park, a way out of masking.

People know their spot on the street. Where we crouch and bend
becomes our house, tent and number. But I squat in mayhem.
Make room of feathers and thread, till day breathes again.

Rain pours down on small and large creatures. So many ill
and then simply passed. But tendrils burst from bough and sky
holds stars before we know what fills us, before time has gone.

Dancers cross ballads, tip singers in bars. But I sit on the curb
watching if one leap becomes another. Bear leaves the forest.
Another tornado. We leave town together; skip the storyline.

No beginning middle or end these days. Hard to plan or know.
Plot might be standing in spring's shadow. What is it we lace
into pockets and dreams, a new rhythm or a closing song?

Spellbound

When the witch cast a spell, she bound the reckless
sex offender to a plate. A bit tighter than she meant,
he lost 30 pounds. Her mixed signals stick and bind.
She sends the crying fool to a seal's cove. Wraps despair
with a hopping rabbit. Roots mania in street tar.

Wish for a lover, find a donkey in the backyard.
Take a lover, he acts more like a donkey than the one
you feed oats to at dawn. (You've taken to the critter).
Pray for a younger body, find a dream full of toddlers.
Glue rhyme to the crisp sleeve of a dull orator.

Breeze opens to a family eating dinner. Three children
stare. One pets a kitten. The parakeet looks up; drops
caraway seeds from a corner cage. Though no one leaned
forward, candles are blown out; soft wind stills the flicker.
Some force keeps the dog, curtain, child hiding behind.

Did the bird sense the cat? He would fly out if the cage
door blew open. Did she wish for stops or starts? Familiar
like a painting, or a story told again and again late at night.
A small girl laughs; knows more than her strapped red
sandals and small bowl of stars intend to share or shine.

The 27 Club

Gray haze, cold in L.A. Not what we are used to.
Fire scars, mud, homes disappearing. More than
25 gone; slipped away before sound or gesture.
Fast as flame licking barn doors down. Fence posts
pointed one way; hope another. Santa Monica Pier,
we ride the Ferris wheel. Bundled in scarf and hat,
you say, "It'd be fun to sleep in this cabin like gulls
in flight." I wonder if we might wake and roll out.
Laughing, you add, "That's like the school teacher
who said two of us would be dead in ten years."
Stunned by this sinister method of teaching stats,
you show the math is right. With facts, simple as
fork and knife, one of your college roommates
passed this year. Nothing in the bulletin, but obit
detailed drugs. "It's the 27 club. Make it to 28,
you live a long time. Not so easy to get there."
Last month, a guy from high school shot himself
in the head when his girl opened the door with
week's poultry and eggs. Who knows if he meant
to pull the trigger right then. "Half the ball team's
gone too. Behind bars or gunned down. Killed for
nothing. And more than two are gone." Slipped
down a different mudslide. We turn round again
between gulls and high waves. Decide to honor
our birthdays at a wild preserve down the road,
with the gibbons. You will turn 28. The gibbons
will sing to each other, bough to bough, cage to
cage. We do the same here, locked in a decade
of silent cries above this gray sea.

Jolt and Smoke

We touch paintings on the wall, each color and pattern a new sky. A face scares you. Your body jumps fast. Legs contract. You scream. The face looks neutral, almost boring. Eyes slightly looking in different directions. On the wall to simply cover a small crack. But this small sculpture is fierce as tiger or jumping knives to you.

A month later, we walk through again. You sight her. Shriek. Bawl. Grandma in Singapore suggests we 'withdraw' the sculpture. Children see ghosts. You saw something active, turning. Wrap her in red paper and place her at base of a tree. I ask why red paper and learn yellow will work as well. Colors of dignity matter.

We make the room and house safe, but also honor the artist and spirit holder. I wrap the silhouette in red satin. We travel to small pond for the new abode. In forest by water, the spirit will know toads, heron waiting for fish tail and egg. Blue jays on bent log. Two deer will look down and up. Swish their small tails.

Not sure where I acquired this clay sculpture. Maybe an art fair or gift from long ago. Her cheeks hold winds; eyes carry pain. Lines run down her neck like a slow moving creek. Clay above her bangs is turban or hill upon her head. We let loose at base of tree, wrapped in fabric. Something beating, a heart or wing. Calm the child. Clear the air.

How do we cover and uncover the claws that clutch us? We bury winds that live inside the chest, that never leave the rattling cage. How does lackluster cause a noise, a shriek, a turning ship? What we see is not all there is. The side lip and turned eye are more than wry. There's smoke inside dreams and winter's cheeks. Something unseen on fire.

Counting, Newtown

Folding on the bed. Gray socks.
A towel. Three shirts. One red,
one blue. An ugly striped mustard.

Pants creased at hip, thigh, calf.
Pajamas with a heart pattern. Wind.
Two sleeping dogs. One cup of coffee.

Two slippers tucked under the bed.
Seven piles of children. Fingers taut.
Holding each other; breath locked in.

Two classrooms. Cheeks touched
shoulders. Knees bent. Huddled.
He shot close. Eleven times.

Nest of wool and wing. Wet and bone.
Nothing left but still. Thirty blue
marbles, a shoelace, one bench.

Running Grace

The boy laughs at blue, abounding
Dust in the air, glitter of fish and tail.

Reaches for spool of threaded color.
Light on wooden floor, short sky, rolling hills.

Walking through loss, through slanted
truth. Where ripple becomes fluster.

What gets us past fence post to wing?
Leafing through darkness, past wind and rhyme.

Ringing stone tucked in fist. Noise hides inside.
The difference between healing and falling.

Words are rocks, one jagged step at a time.
When did harmony become a knife?

Bee to clover as knee to soft prayer.
The sky tips over; light blue in his hands.

In Line for COVID Kits and Masks

Teens slide an incline by the road. Traffic stopped. Snow piles up. An American flag smacks the wind rough, back and forth; sounds like a door coming off its hinges. Cops cropped in gold vests against the cold, wave florescent orange traffic sticks. We thread along in cars for miles like a coiled serpent on the road.

Turn in to the middle school. A child sweeps the glass hillside in silver snowsuit. Her parents watch. The sky, pale blue and white, almost dreamlike. Fallen trees by the creek, from the last storm. Torn bags hang from branches in random design, crafted by flood and winds at night when even those who rake and brush don't see what floats away.

We can't turn around. Row of cars for six miles, broken into five lines. Give in to this pace of day, waiting for two masks and test kits, the size and weight of a mitten. From another decade, the school sign reads Tobacco Free Zone. Concert gazebo painted thick in ice. Snow falls off roofs as sun flares down. Stairs lead to empty classrooms.

Moms quit their jobs. Won't look back. Who can file, hug and teach with just two hands and a clock? We turn wheels slowly and together in thick soot. Almost an intentional meditation. Footprints go nowhere in snow fields we watch. Ground brushed white, brings calm surprise to the restless, waiting for stronger masks and kits that barely work.

Try this test three times in a row over a few days to be sure you're virus-free. We learn patience and trials. Some will die. Some will never feel quite right again. This time children take ill which drives a crude knife into the path we wait on for our turn in fate and fairness. So many seniors gone, too. Toddlers wear masks all day in pre-school.

Some tiny ones have trouble taking air in and out. They said this would not happen. A few downed, like these thin saplings in the storm. Owls hoot in both day and night, as if no one's listening. Meaning has turned over, our language changed. No beginning middle or end, anymore. Hope is a split road now; roots are tearing fast.

Hostage

When memory and promise are one
facts tack on like hangers and nails.
Fibs become lies. Lies become
blankets. Everyone is lying down.

In Paris, weathered vanes and eaves
point south. Geese letter the sky.
A son bikes home a basket of candles,
quince and fresh marzipan.

When memory and promise are one
trees shake down small boys.
The sleepless start laughing.
What rattles a thin-boned cage?

When memory and promise are one
dogs bark on, as if locked in warning.
The family's front porch seems long
gone, but poke a thin joke slowly.

She irons a long gray dress.
The heat hides lies and wrinkles in
a complex time. Memory is a lost silk
slip, as winds turn a restless hunger.

When memory and promise are one,
sharp hymns tear the skin.
The kosher store means nothing at all
until they call it the Jewish store.

Then the shooting begins.
Nailed to memory, blankets of promise.
The joke is in the basket.
Everyone is lying down.

Orienteering

Activity in which you find your way with map & compass,
between checkpoints on unfamiliar terrain, moving at speed.

She fled through broken window fractured
screams, alone. Miles of hillside wet clothes
shoes crumpled. Tents at end without water.
Some acts of kindness. A rag doll to hug, tuck in.
Up and down noises like cries, but they weren't.

No one knows what words are, until they disappear.
Worse than missing teeth, the gaping inside.
Refugee school is next to the one for slow learners.
They call her war refugee, not immigrant. Welcome
for a little while; but don't take off your coat.

She mimics nonchalance. Walks without pause,
though loss is a blackbird flying home without her.
She knows what hovers. Wings show in small gestures—
the flick of a hand, empty eyes when streets wind
far or fire breaks through a long horizon.

Her class roams the landscape with map and pushpins.
Can they read unknown terrain, swiftly walk through
pine forests? She moves from one map to another.
Knows that destiny is not in the tracing of lines, but in
hiding between them. Silence of bodies holding still.

Carrying her life in her hands. She could feel their nails,
laughter, the blood. Nothing went away, not even in math
class or chorus singing by the organ with the others.
Maybe some of them, also. No one talked about it;
just singing hymns. Leave quietly. Don't stay in line.

She drowns her tastes, her tongue. Traces new words.
Linnaeus—known for sorting animals and plants.
Lagom—not too little, not too much.
Kajuna—thousands of blackbirds turning wingtip to sky.
Orienteer-finding the way through loss, through limbs.

Between Words

silt *hair*	Silk sheath. Falling laugh, leaves, rain.
absolve *simple*	Stains washed away. Clean shirt hanging dry.
under *foul*	How it really went down. He pressed forward.
tip *crimson*	Tulip dropped petals. Nothing remaining but seed.
flight *pause*	What if she stays? She bends to gather time.
dreams *ghost*	Warning of something other than loss.
black out *alley*	Car at the curb. She forgot how she arrived.
cop *missing*	Nothing but a look. Neighbors spew plot.
wander *tilt*	Fox next to her. Smelling between words.
forgive *forget*	The liar leans forward.
hearth *rattle*	Circle the prayers; rattle the soul.
whisper *round*	Light ebbs blue. Angels spin.

Speeding By, Still

Eagle flies to the sandbar twice a day. Others line up on
tall oak that lays flat, toppled in spring's fiercest storm.
They look out together, raven, blue heron, crow. We peer
at them through dense forest and fenced path. A parade
of who's who, separated by town's water. Deer amble
out to patches of gold light. Test summer greens and pink
nasturtium. Perched on roof's tip, gray squirrel watches.

Fearless rabbits chew garden kale, lounge on lawn and
walkways. Sometimes they freeze, as if to disappear.
But the ins and outs of breath give them away. Nearby,
pesticide may have undone some chipmunks, flat out on
sloped grass. Cars at night often robbed. Leave change in
sight, windows may be smashed by dawn. An older woman's
head banged against concrete at the shopping center.

Thrown in the back of her car with two bags of groceries.
They sped away fast. Is this shared despair among youth
or new-found bravery? Car abandoned on the freeway.
She's in the backseat, waiting for something to be undone,
untied. Growing mayhem. Start over, begin again. Swans try
to nest at the sandbar two years in a row. Lose what they built.
How were they to sense the ebb and swell of rain and storm?

No one knows what will be gone, ripped by germ, winds or
hand. We're stuck inside fears of Covid for so long. Nature
comes closer, further in. Rats nest under car hoods. Gnaw
through wires. Bears rummage in trash, enter back doors.
Finally, we push open windows and look after loss. Masks
off, what will be taken next? We don't know the questions
to ask so many gone and now the trees are on fire.

Drought

Fewer wetlands, drought thins wing and flight.
Birds leave their nests. Eggs swept by wind.
Streams stop flowing. Fish no longer cascade down.
Who can protect when nothing endures?

Birds leave their nests. Eggs swept by wind.
The heart is often empty.
Who can protect when nothing endures?
Bugs and mice dig in to earth.

The heart is often empty.
Sky vast with stars. Some will fall.
Bugs and mice dig in to earth
Even the horses lie down.

Sky vast with stars. Some will fall.
What was ripe is dry, hay piled up.
Even the horses lie down.
Shallow warm water. Disease spreads fast.

What was ripe is dry, hay piled up.
Hungry for wing and wet.
Shallow warm water. Disease spreads fast.
There is little green beneath us.

Hungry for wing and wet.
What's missing leads to thirst.
There is little green beneath us.
Sky, the new river, moves blue and fast.

Reading of Entrails & Other Items

If the coils of the colon of the sacrificial lamb
are like the crescent of the moon,
then the ruler of the army will have no rivals.
           Peabody Museum, Babylonian Collection

If the pond reflects firs and
firs reflect sky, then the woman
who sees before and beyond,
will leave you.

If lust knows edge in alleys
like ermine and fox on the prowl,
then roads will swerve round
and the compass will fail.

If the hound pants up the hill
like a horn chasing notes,
then the body will tremble
and the hand reach for more.

If shutter bangs against stone,
like hammers in the mine,
then memory will pound,
loud clatter in the veins.

If shadow and echo are friends
in the day, like owl and wolf
at night, then moon will light
the lone man, walking.

If crow takes the shell and flies
away, like the lies you lift when
pained, then the body of the catch
will fall down fast, go missing.

If laughter turns raucous
like nightcaps at dawn,
then words will spill letters;
make poems of us all.

ACKNOWLEDGMENTS

The following poems have appeared in magazines, anthologies and newspapers, sometimes in earlier versions. Grateful acknowledgment is made to the editors.

Connecticut Literary Anthology: "Drought"
Valiant Scribe: "Pandemic Spring and the What?"
US1 Worksheets: "Found," Volume 67, DVP/US1 Poets
CT Poetry Society: "Lullaby During Insurrection," Nutmeg Award
Quiet Diamonds: "To a Survivor"
Dillydoun Review: "Last Ten Days of August"
Encore Magazine: "Spellbound," Power of Women Award, "Counting Newtown," William Stafford Memorial Award
Stories That Need to Be Told: "On My Way to Coffee During Covid"
Quiet Diamonds: "Cold Know-How"
Hartford Courant, CT Poets Corner: "Echo of Stone," "The Ditch," "The 27 Club"
Take a Stand: Art Against Hate Anthology: "Echo of Stone"
101 Jewish Poems for the Third Millennium: "Hostage"
Connecticut River Review: "The Ditch," CT Poetry Award; "Echo of Stone"
Adanna Literary Review, Women and War: "What Was Left"
Americas Review: #14, Writing of the Political Movements: "Orienteering"

Gifts of my writer's group ribbon through these pages. Thanks to Ginny Connors, Julia Paul, Sherri Bedingfield, Nancy Kerrigan, Pat Hale, Joan Hoffman, Debbie Gilbert and Christine Beck. My family brings art and invention to the dinner table. Love to Hannah, Ben, Yen, Naomi and my husband, David Plotke. Marilyn Kallet, my sister, is forever the mentor.

Elaine Zimmerman writes poetry, policy, and curriculum. Her poems have been published in anthologies, newspapers, social policy communications and journals as well as two chapbooks. She writes on the unexpected and often on unsettling events. Her work is riddled with a subtle beauty and she unearths hope.

Her background includes work for both state legislatures and the federal government. She has launched non-profits for children and families and successful state and national initiatives. Over four decades, she has led on poverty reduction, equity, school success and parent leadership.

Her organizing and policy design often bring the power of art and language forward. Children and youth are invited to share their ideas through writing and illustration. Readings and exhibits pop up of youth speaking on Newtown, 9/11, Katrina, and/or bullying. She helps storyteller meet storyteller and builds social capital among those who share hopes and narratives.

Her work in policy is often broken open with a poem or a story, to get to the heart of the matter. Her belief in the power of language to heal and inform is foremost. Strength of civic voice emerges in her coalescing of youth and family stories to improve systems.

Elaine has received honors in poetry and policy. These include an honorary Women in Government Award from *Good Housekeeping Magazine* and the U.S. Secretary's Meritorious Service Award. She is a Pushcart nominee and recent recipient of the Nutmeg Poetry and William Stafford awards.